This book belongs to:
_____

Goodnight Trump
Copyright © 2016 by Antonio Carter
All rights reserved. No part of this publication may be reproduced, distributed, or transmitted in any form or by any means, including photocopying, recording, or other electronic or mechanical methods, without the prior written permission of the publisher, except in the case of brief quotations embodied in critical reviews and certain other noncommercial uses permitted.

Goodnight Trump

In this lavish bedroom
There was a table
And a ratty toupee
And a painting of...

And a washed up child star who was not gone too soon.

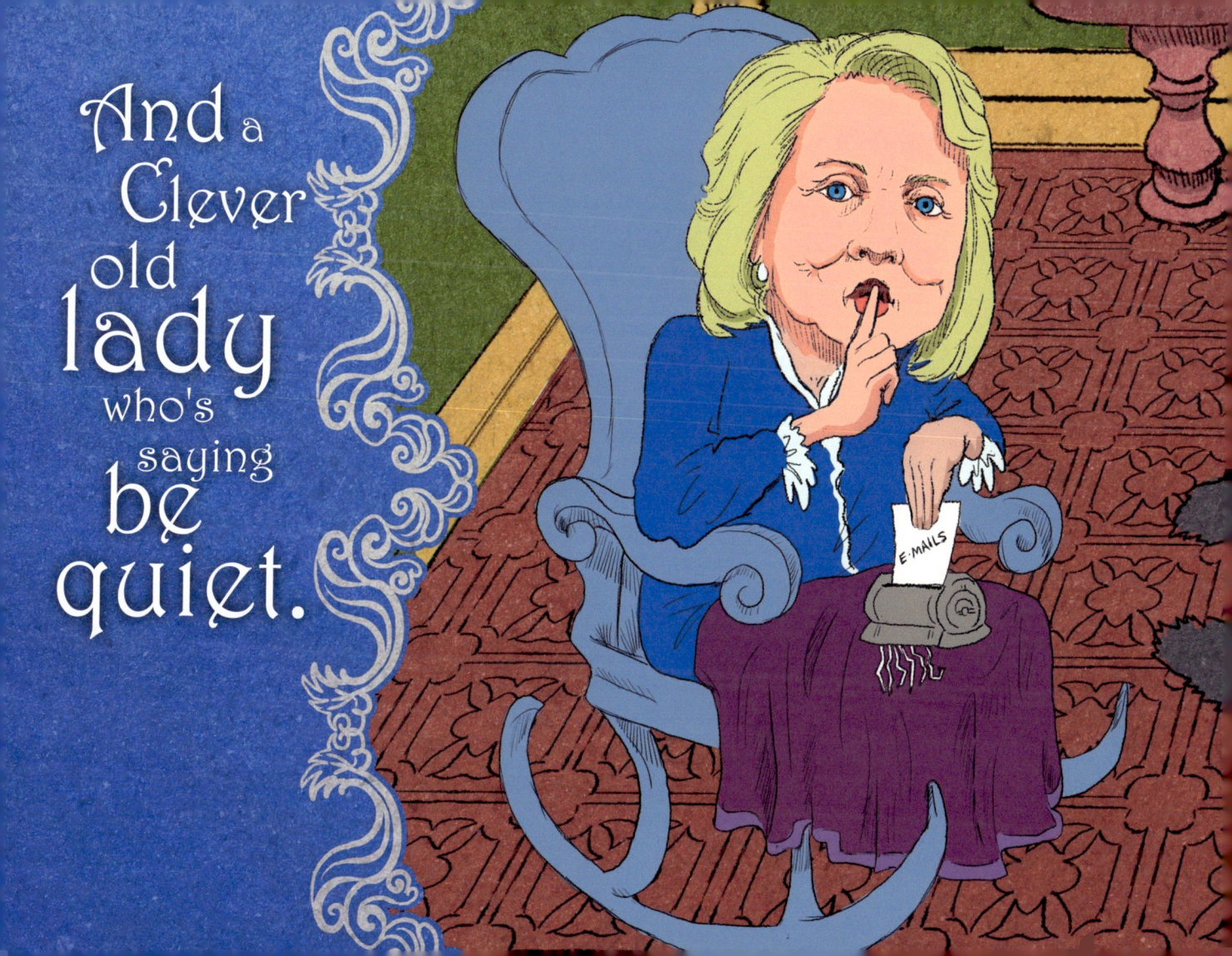

Goodnight painting of Donald in tight gold lamé'.

Goodnight Trump's rude and racist Supporters. No more talks of violence or Mexican borders.

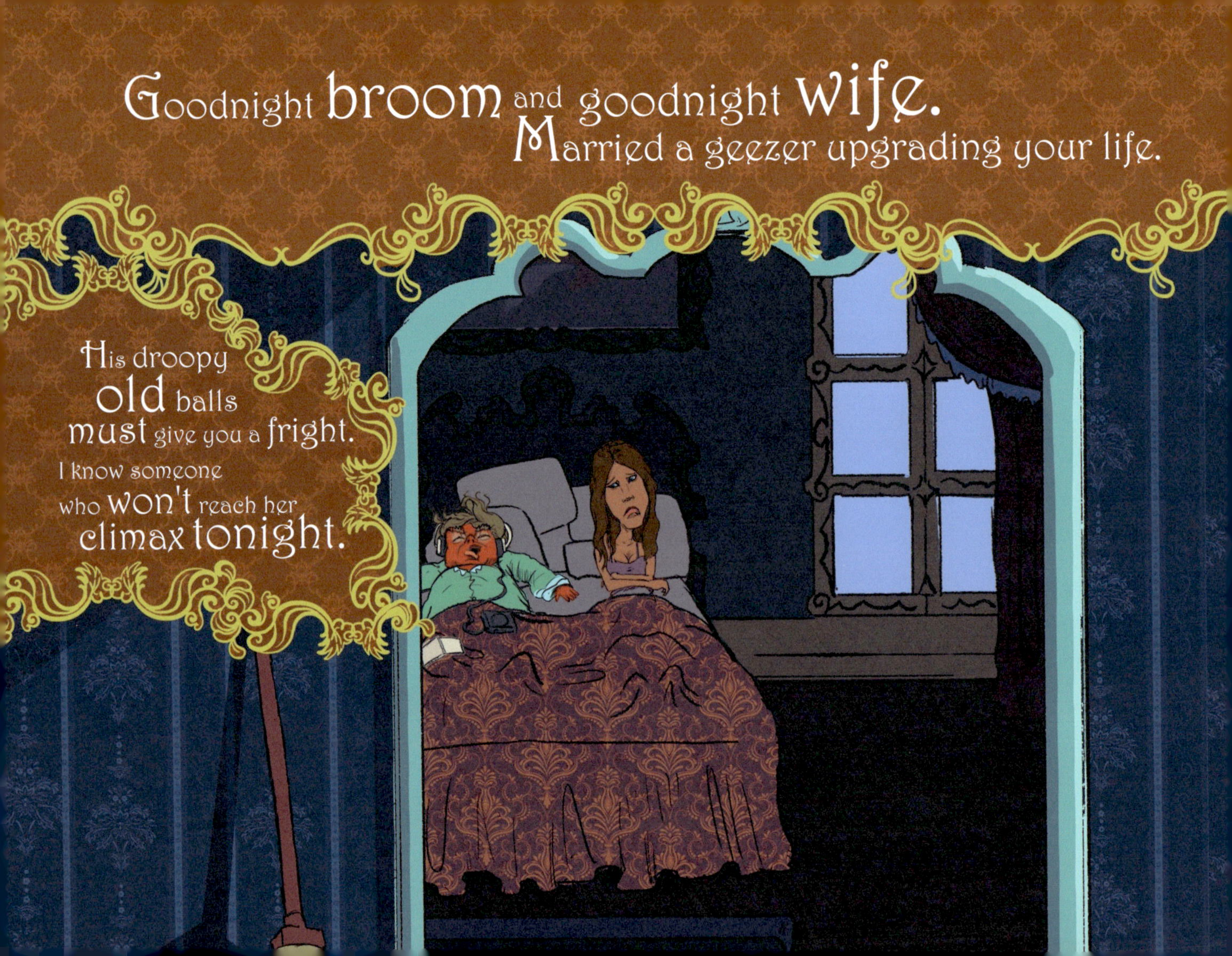

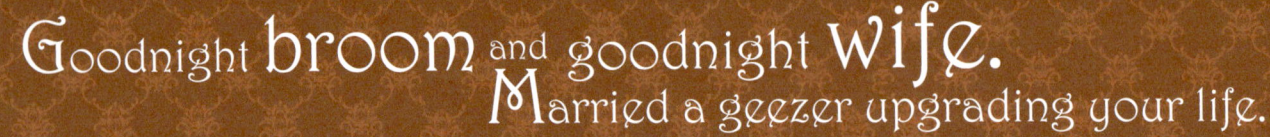

Made in the USA
Columbia, SC
21 May 2025